THE TIMING WOUND

Sacred Return and the End of Perpetual Offering

KRISTI HALL

GRIST

THE TIMING WOUND
SACRED RETURN AND THE END OF PERPETUAL OFFERING

GRIST
United States · Second Edition

The God does not remain crowned.

He rises, governs, offers, and returns.

And in his turning, the world is renewed.

CONTENTS

Preface vii

Introduction xiii

PART I   1

Chapter 1: The Wheel as Cosmology 3

Chapter 2: The Four Seasons 7

Chapter 3: Many Wheels at Once 21

PART II   31

Chapter 4: The Burnout That Doesn't Respond to Rest 33

Chapter 5: The Collapse of Sacred Time 37

Chapter 6: Premature Sacrifice 43

PART III   49

Chapter 7: Finding Your Current Season 51

Chapter 8: Repairing the Timeline 55

Chapter 9: The Rhythm Rule 61

Chapter 10: The Personal Wheel Plan 67

Chapter 11: When the Wheel Doesn't Fit 71

Chapter 12: The Return You Keep 77

Appendix A: The Season Finder 81

Appendix B: Two Completed Personal Wheel Plans 83

Appendix C: The Weekly Wheel Ledger 87

Appendix D: The Closing Rite and Vow of Timing 89

Appendix E: Works in Conversation 91

Continuing the Work 93

About the Author 95

Why This Book Uses Pagan Gods to Talk About Burnout

I want to tell you how I arrived at the framework in this book, because the path matters. If you are not Pagan—if you have never celebrated a solstice, never heard of the Wheel of the Year, never given a second thought to what ancient European people believed about their gods—this book is still for you. But you deserve to know why I am asking you to think about burnout in the context of these particular stories.

Like many people, I arrived at this framework the hard way: through exhaustion. I had been tired for years—not the kind of tired that sleep fixes, but the kind that waits for you on the other side of every vacation, every boundary, every attempt at self-care. I had read the burnout books. I had tried the strategies. Some helped. None reached the thing underneath.

What eventually reached it was a story about a god who dies on purpose.

A Different Story About Time

Most of us were raised inside a particular story about time, whether we recognize it or not. In the dominant Western framework—shaped by centuries of industrial capitalism and, before that, by certain strands of Christian theology—time is linear. It moves forward. Progress is the goal.

Productivity is the proof of a life well lived. Rest is a reward you earn, not a season you enter. And giving—of your time, your energy, your labor, your love—is treated as an essentially unlimited obligation. The more you give, the better you are.

This story is so pervasive that it feels like reality rather than a story. But it is a story. And there are others.

Contemporary Paganism—a broad family of spiritual traditions rooted in pre-Christian European practices, seasonal observation, and relationship with the natural world—carries a fundamentally different story about time. In the Pagan imagination, time is not a line. It is a wheel. The year turns through seasons with different qualities, different demands, and different gifts. There are times to act and times to be still. Times to give and times to withdraw. Times to be visible and times to disappear. The turning itself is sacred—not just the productive parts.

This is not merely a metaphor for "go with the flow" or "take a break sometimes." It is a fully articulated cosmology—a way of understanding what life requires to remain viable over time. And at the center of that cosmology, in many Pagan traditions, is a story about what the gods themselves do with power.

THE GOD WHO DESCENDS

Within the Wheel of the Year—an eightfold cycle marked by solstices, equinoxes, and the cross-quarter festivals between them—many practitioners tell a story about the God's journey through the year. The details differ by tradition, but the underlying movement is remarkably consistent:

He begins in hiddenness. He grows. He comes into strength and takes his place as a sovereign, generative force. He gives of himself—not endlessly, but in a timed, consecrated offering. And then he descends. He withdraws. He disappears. He enters the dark. And from that darkness, he returns.

This arc—which I call Becoming, Authority, Offering, and Return—is not a quaint fairy tale. It is a theological claim about the nature of power: that power is seasonal, that giving has a right time, and an end, and that withdrawal is not failure but part of the sacred design.

When I first looked at my own burnout through this lens, something shifted. I was not merely stressed. I was not merely overworked. I was living in perpetual Offering—giving without a gate, without an end, without any structural permission to descend. My culture had taught me that endurance was a virtue and visibility was proof of worth. The God's arc suggested something different: that the willingness to disappear—to stop producing, stop being available, stop performing—might be the most sacred thing you could do.

WHY PAGAN TIME HELPS WHERE OTHER FRAMEWORKS DON'T

If you come from an organized religious background, you may have encountered sabbath theology the idea that rest is commanded, that one day in seven belongs to God, that you are not your productivity. These traditions carry real wisdom. But they often frame rest as obedience to a divine command from above, and they tend to leave the underlying story of time intact: time is still linear, still moving toward a final destination, and rest is an interruption of the real business of living.

Pagan seasonal theology does something structurally different. It does not interrupt linear time with rest. It replaces linear time with cyclical time.

In the Wheel's cosmology, withdrawal is not a pause in the story. It is part of the story. Descent is not a break from the sacred. It is the sacred. The God does not rest from his work. He completes his arc—and the arc includes darkness, concealment, and the dissolution of everything he built.

This matters for burnout because most burned-out people do not simply need a break. They need a different story about what time is for. They need permission that goes deeper than "you deserve rest"—permission that is built into the structure of the cosmos rather than granted as a concession. The Wheel of the Year offers that permission. Not as a command from above, but as a pattern observed in the turning of the world itself.

You do not have to be Pagan to find this useful. You do not have to believe in the God as a literal being. What the framework asks is simpler: that you consider the possibility that your life has seasons, that those seasons have different requirements, and that honoring those requirements—rather than overriding them with sheer will—might be the thing your exhaustion has been asking for all along.

WHAT THIS BOOK IS—AND WHAT IT ISN'T

I am not a priest. I am not a therapist. I am a person who has practiced Pagan spirituality for many years and who noticed something: the seasonal mythology I had been living with contained a remarkably precise diagnosis of the specific kind of exhaustion that modern life produces. The more I explored that diagnosis, the more it became clear in my life.

This book is my attempt to share that framework clearly enough to be useful. It draws on the Wheel of the Year, on the God's mythic journey, and on my own experience of applying this lens to burnout, boundaries, and the problem of living in a world that treats perpetual giving as proof of worth. It is offered as a heuristic—a way of seeing what modern time has hidden from view—not as doctrine, not as clinical treatment, and not as the final word on anything.

If it helps, use it. If parts of it don't fit your life, trust that. I am not handing down a system you must follow perfectly. I am describing a pattern I have found genuinely useful and inviting you to see whether it illuminates anything in your own experience.

. . .

The chapters that follow explore what happens when the God's seasonal pattern is distorted—and what may be restored when it is remembered. You will find a diagnosis, a framework, and a set of practical tools. You will also find, I hope, a different kind of permission: the permission to stop offering from a place that has run dry, and to come back into season.

THE TIMING WOUND

Burnout is usually treated as a problem of stress, resilience, or personal limitation. You are told to sleep more, set boundaries, manage your nervous system, change your mindset, find balance.

Some of this helps. Much of it does not—especially when the exhaustion you are living with does not resolve through rest alone.

There is a fatigue that returns the moment you resume your life. A depletion that feels not only physical but moral and spiritual—because it carries the suspicion that you are failing at something fundamental. Failing to endure. Failing to keep up. Failing to give without limit.

This kind of burnout does not feel like tiredness. It feels like misalignment. It feels like living in the wrong season.

This book begins with that recognition. Burnout is not only overwork. It is often mis-timing—a disruption of seasonal order. It is what happens when a life is pressed to remain in one phase of its arc long after that phase has fulfilled its purpose.

...

In Wheel of the Year cosmology, the God does not remain in one state. He is born in concealment. He grows in hiddenness. He comes into strength. He takes the crown. He gives himself to the land. He descends. He disappears. He returns.

This movement reveals a pattern of continuity. Becoming protects what is forming. Authority stabilizes and governs. Offering gives what is ripe. Return restores what has been spent.

The seed is not harvested. The fruit is not demanded in winter. The field lies fallow not as failure but as necessity. Living systems endure because they move within this order. When that order is disrupted, life becomes strained.

• • •

A NOTE ON THE GODDESS

Some readers will notice that this book centers on the God's arc exclusively. This is a deliberate choice, but it deserves explanation.

The Goddess's journey through the Wheel is its own theology—one of sovereignty, transformation, descent, and return that carries its own power. Her arc is not secondary to his; it is complementary, and in many traditions, it is the deeper story. A full treatment of her seasonal movement deserves its own book, written with the same care and specificity.

This book centers on the God's arc because his particular pattern—the rise into visible authority, the consecrated offering, the chosen descent—maps with unusual precision onto the specific shape of modern burnout. The cultural demand to remain crowned, remain productive, remain visible, remain giving—these are distortions of a masculine mythic pattern, and they affect people of all genders. The God's arc names this distortion clearly.

But the Goddess is not absent from these pages. She appears wherever sovereignty appears, wherever the land's own intelligence is honored, wherever the question shifts from "what must I give?" to "what does the living world actually require?" Her presence is the reason the Wheel turns at all. Without her, the God's arc would be a straight line—and straight lines do not renew.

Burnout emerges when we imitate only part of the arc. We accept the crown but not the descent. We accept responsibility but not concealment. We accept offering but resist return. Modern life encourages permanence in Authority and Offering. It asks for steadiness without interruption, for productivity without threshold, for visibility without disappearance.

This distortion has a name: premature sacrifice.

Premature sacrifice is an offering that has not reached readiness. It is giving from the seed rather than from the harvest. It is mistaking depletion for devotion. It often feels noble, necessary, even responsible. But the God's offering is timed. His descent is bounded.

His return is assured. A gift that empties the giver past viability is not sacred. It is extraction.

You do not heal burnout by becoming more resilient inside a distorted structure. You heal burnout by restoring seasonal alignment.

This book offers a theology of burnout as seen through the God's journey across the year. It treats myth not as ornament, but as architecture. Part One names the pattern — the fourfold arc of Becoming, Authority, Offering, and Return — and shows how it applies to the overlapping domains of adult life. Part Two names the wound: what happens when that pattern is disrupted, when sacred time collapses, and when offering is demanded before it is ripe.

Part Three offers a way back — not a program, but a practice of locating yourself within the season you are actually living.

This is not a productivity system in sacred language.

You are not asked to optimize your seasons or perform the Wheel correctly. This is not medical or therapeutic treatment. Exhaustion may arise from grief, trauma, depression, anxiety, chronic illness, or systemic harm. A sacred framework should illuminate reality, not conceal it.

A word of care: if your exhaustion is accompanied by persistent hopelessness, thoughts of self-harm, an inability to feel anything at all, or a sense that you are in danger—from yourself or from someone in your life—this book is not enough. Please seek support from a licensed therapist or counselor. The Wheel can work alongside professional care. It is not designed to replace it. There is no sacred framework that should ever be used to delay the help you need right now.

What this book insists upon is simpler: Return is not indulgence. It is not weakness. It is not reward. It is part of the design.

The year turns. The God descends and rises again. If you are willing to re-enter that pattern—not perfectly, not dramatically, but honestly—burnout can become what it was always trying to be: a summons. Not to strive harder. But to come back into season.

PART I

The God's Arc

CHAPTER 1

THE WHEEL AS COSMOLOGY

Before we can name what is broken, we need to understand what wholeness looks like — not as an ideal, but as a pattern. The Wheel of the Year carries that pattern, and it makes a claim that modern time cannot easily absorb: that life is not a line. It is an arc that turns, and the turning is not optional.

This is not a book about seasonal living in the general sense — not an invitation to match your wardrobe to autumn or your playlist to winter. This book is built on a stricter claim: the Wheel of the Year carries a pattern of viable life, and that pattern — expressed through the God's arc — is the structure that makes repair possible.

In Wheel cosmology, the God does not remain in one condition. He becomes, he ripens into authority, he offers, he dies, he returns. The story is cosmological: it describes what life requires to remain viable over time. It insists on gates. It insists that offering must be followed by return. It insists that what is unformed must be protected, and what is ripe must be released, and what has been spent must be restored.

NOT AESTHETIC, NOT HOBBY

For many people, the Wheel of the Year has become lifestyle language: seasonal décor, self-care playlists, rituals as content. None of this is inherently wrong. People are hungry for rhythm, and even a shallow contact with season can feel like relief.

But when the Wheel is treated as aesthetic, it becomes optional—something you do when you have time. And if it is optional, it cannot heal what we have been naming. You cannot repair the collapse of sacred time with a decorative version of sacred time.

What is needed is not seasonal content, but seasonal pattern. A cosmology is not a theme. It is a description of what living systems require to remain viable. The Wheel, approached this way, makes a serious claim: life moves in arcs, viability depends on timing, and renewal is not a reward—it is part of the structure.

THE FOURFOLD ORDER

The God's journey can be named as four seasons in human life:

Becoming — what is forming, concealed, gestating; the discipline of protection and restraint.

Authority — what is stable, governed, held in continuity; the discipline of limits and stewardship.

Offering — what is ripe, outward, given; the discipline of clean release without depletion.

Return — what is withdrawn, fallow, darkened, restored; the discipline of disappearance and renewal.

Notice what this arc does not include: constant visibility, constant output, constant optimization, constant sacrifice. It includes sacrifice, yes—but it is seasoned, gated, rightly timed. The God offers when he is ripe, and the offering is followed by Return.

GATES, NOT GOALS

One of the most important shifts in this book is this: the Wheel is not a set of goals. It is a set of gates. A goal says: achieve this, prove this, complete this. A gate says: this is the condition you are in; behave accordingly.

When you are in Becoming, the gate says: Protect.

Do not force.

When you are in Authority, the gate says: Govern. Choose limits.

When you are in Offering, the gate says: Give cleanly. End it.

When you are in Return, the gate says: Withdraw. Restore. Disappear.

The Wheel is not asking you to become a better person. It is inviting you to stop violating time.

Each Season Can Be Distorted

The Wheel is not moralizing. It is ordering. Each season is sacred when it is rightly lived. Each season becomes costly when it is distorted.

Becoming becomes stagnation when it refuses ripening.

Authority becomes tyranny when it refuses humility and return.

Offering becomes martyrdom when it refuses gates.

Return becomes avoidance when it refuses eventual re-entry.

The point is not to idealize any one phase. The point is to restore movement. Burnout often feels like being trapped in one posture. The Wheel offers an exit because it reminds you that time is allowed to turn.

The Theology Beneath the System

At the heart of this cosmology is a theological claim that modern time struggles to tolerate:

Not everything is supposed to be visible.

Not everything is supposed to be productive. Not everything is supposed to be offered.

Some things are meant to be protected until they can survive. Some offerings are meant to be made once and then released. Some seasons are meant to be dark.

The sacred does not only live in what you give. It also lives in what you withhold, what you protect, what you restore, what you refuse to force.

· · ·

REFLECTION

Where have you treated the Wheel as aesthetic rather than as a pattern of life?

Where in your life have you been pushed into perpetual kingship or perpetual offering, with Return treated as illegitimate?

Which season feels most illegitimate to you: Becoming, Authority, Offering, or Return? Why?

If the Wheel is a set of gates rather than goals, what gate are you currently ignoring?

CHAPTER 2

THE FOUR SEASONS

The first season the modern world tries to steal from you is Becoming. Not because Becoming is unimportant, but because Becoming is difficult to monetize, measure, and display.

Becoming asks for viability. In the God's arc, Becoming is not a prelude you rush through on the way to real life. It is a necessary condition: the hidden season in which form is gathered, promise is protected, and life is allowed to take shape without being demanded to serve too early.

Becoming is not doing. Becoming is forming. And what is forming must be protected.

One of the deepest wounds modern time inflicts is the suspicion of hiddenness. If something is not visible, it is treated as not real. If something is not productive, it is treated as not valuable.

Becoming contradicts this. It insists that the unseen is not empty—it is gestational. It is the place where life gathers its strength before it risks exposure.

The discipline of Becoming is restraint—not withholding out of fear, but withholding out of timing. It is the decision to protect what is forming from the demand for immediate clarity, immediate output, immediate proof, and immediate usefulness. It is the act of refusing to hand your seed to a world that only knows how to harvest.

Signs you are in Becoming: a quiet inner pressure of something forming but not yet coherent. You are drawn toward something, but your language for it keeps shifting. You are learning and absorbing more than producing. You feel tender, easily overwhelmed, or protective of your inner life. Visibility feels destabilizing rather than exciting. These are not defects. They are cues.

THE GOD IN BECOMING

In the Wheel's mythology, the God at Imbolc is the Uncrowned Heir. His light has returned since Yule—the direction of the year has shifted, the descent has ended—and yet nothing in the visible world confirms his presence. The ground remains hard. The cold persists. Growth is not evident. He exists before he is convincing.

He is promise without proof.

Modern imagination often equates masculine power with assertion. Imbolc offers a different measure.

Here, strength is steadiness. Authority is not absent; it is taking shape. The heir lives. The lineage is secure. But the crown remains unworn. This waiting is not denial; it is maturation. Power exercised too soon can exhaust itself. Authority claimed before it has met resistance becomes brittle.

The God at Imbolc must learn something more difficult than conquest: he must learn to inhabit duration—to remain aligned with return without demanding recognition. Authority that endures is shaped in obscurity long before it is tested in light.

If you are in Becoming and you feel like a fraud—unproven, invisible, unable to point to results—remember this: the God himself stood uncrowned. That was not his failure. That was the season working.

AUTHORITY

Authority is the season that follows Becoming—not as a reward, but as a consequence. When something has been given time to form, it can be governed.

When something has matured enough to stand, it can be held in continuity.

In the Wheel's cosmology, kingship is not a personality trait. It is a condition: the steady phase of the God's arc in which what has become viable is now sustained, ordered, and protected from chaos. Authority is what makes the rest of the arc possible. Without Authority, offerings become impulsive.

Without Authority, Return becomes collapse rather than intentional withdrawal.

Modern culture has taught many people a counterfeit version of authority—one that looks like constant competence, relentless productivity, and unbroken availability. That counterfeit is part of the burnout mechanism. It turns stewardship into strain. True Authority feels different from performance. It is quieter. It does not need to be seen to be real. It is not frantic. Authority is the difference between being busy and being ordered, between being needed and being governed, between being competent and being sovereign.

The simplest definition of Authority: it is what preserves continuity. It means the household runs without you carrying every detail in your nervous system. It means your commitments are survivable. Authority reduces the cost of living by replacing chaos with structure.

In Authority, boundaries are not walls—they are gates. A gate says: this is when we stop, this is what I can offer, this is what I cannot carry. Authority is the season where you learn to end things on purpose.

But Authority becomes distorted when it is severed from Return. Governance becomes control. Limits become rigidity. The Wheel does not sanctify a life that is technically in order but spiritually dead.

Authority is sacred when it remains humble enough to turn.

THE GOD IN AUTHORITY

At Midsummer, the God stands crowned. Light reaches its height. He is sovereign—visible, radiant, fully expressed. The world answers his vitality. The land greens. Life unfolds in abundance. This is the God at the peak of his arc: powerful, generative, holding a world in order.

But even at the summit, the Wheel carries a whisper of turning. Midsummer is not only fullness—it is the first signal that decline will follow. The longest day contains within it the knowledge that days will shorten. The God does not panic at this. He does not clutch the crown. He governs knowing that governance is temporary, that the crown is held in trust, not owned.

This is the discipline of Authority: to hold power without believing it is permanent. To govern without confusing stewardship with identity. The crowned God does not say, "I am the crown." He says, "The crown is mine to carry for this season."

When you are in Authority—when your work is steady, your household is ordered, your competence is visible—the temptation is to believe that this is who you are. That the stability is you, that the governance is your identity, that stepping back from it would mean losing yourself. The God at Midsummer teaches otherwise: you can be fully sovereign and still know that the season will turn. That knowledge is not a threat. It is what keeps Authority honest.

Authority is not the moment when effort ends. It is the moment when effort changes form.

In Becoming, energy gathers toward a center. In Authority, that center must hold under weight.

This is the season in which what formed in hiddenness becomes responsible for something beyond itself. The God no longer protects only his own viability. He protects a world that now depends on his steadiness. Crops grow beneath his light.

Households organize around his rhythm. His presence is no longer private. It is infrastructural.

Authority is not the freedom to act without constraint. It is the obligation to remain coherent so that others may live within the order you sustain.

This is why Authority can feel both powerful and heavy.

The modern world often treats Authority as a reward for effort — a position you earn and then enjoy. In the Wheel's cosmology, Authority is not a reward. It is an assignment. It asks you to remain when leaving would be easier. It asks you to repeat what is necessary even when it is no longer exciting. It asks you to hold structures in place long enough for life to mature within them.

Authority is the season of maintenance.

This maintenance is not glamorous. It is rhythmic. Cyclical. Often invisible. It lives in the daily acts that preserve continuity: paying the bills, answering the messages, showing up for the people and systems that now rely on your presence. Authority means that your absence carries consequence.

This is why Authority is the phase most easily distorted into burnout.

Burnout often does not begin in Becoming. It begins in Authority, when governance loses its rhythm and becomes constant vigilance. When the one who governs forgets that the Wheel turns, Authority hardens into permanence. The crowned God becomes a tyrant not because he sought power, but because he forgot that power was seasonal.

The Wheel protects against this distortion by placing Authority between Becoming and Offering.

Authority is never the destination. It is the phase in which power learns how to carry responsibility without consuming itself.

The God at Midsummer demonstrates this discipline not through conquest, but through endurance. He rises each day and crosses the sky. He does not accelerate to prove himself. He does not burn out. His Authority lies in his consistency. Life flourishes not because he is dramatic, but because he is reliable.

Reliability is the deepest expression of Authority.

It allows others to root, to grow, to risk their own Becoming under the shelter of something stable.

But even as he governs, the God remains aware of the turning.

Authority is not his identity. It is his office.

He knows that what he sustains now, he will one day release. This knowledge does not weaken his governance. It refines it. He does not extract everything he can from the season. He preserves what must survive beyond him.

This is the sacred paradox of Authority:

You must carry fully what you know you cannot keep.

This is what makes Authority sustainable rather than consumptive. It is governance in relationship with time.

And this is why Authority, properly held, does not exhaust the soul.

It stabilizes it.

Authority becomes wounding only when you are asked to govern without rhythm, to sustain without relief, to carry without Return.

When Authority is aligned with the Wheel, it does not trap you. It gives your life structure strong enough to hold your Offering and gentle enough to release you when your season turns.

OFFERING

Offering is the season people most often mistake for virtue. Not because offering is wrong—offering is part of the God's arc, part of what makes life meaningful—but because collapsed time trains us to treat giving as proof.

Right-timed offering is not continuous giving. It is a consecrated release that has a gate. In the God's arc, Offering is not the whole year. It is a season that arrives when ripeness is present—when Becoming has formed substance, and Authority has created a container strong enough to hold the gift.

A sacred offering has four qualities:

Ripeness: It comes from what has matured. Even when it is humble, it carries a sense of completion: this can be given without destroying what must continue.

Choice: It is chosen, not extracted. If the yes is only fear, the offering has already become premature sacrifice.

A gate: It has an end, a closure, a boundary. A consecrated time when the giving is complete and you are released.

Clean release: It is given without attaching your worth to the outcome. Offered, and then let go.

Offering is a spiritual act because it is the moment when what has been formed is released outward into relationship—into community, into the world, into life. But if you attempt to circulate what has not matured, you will circulate depletion. Right-timed offering circulates life. Mis-timed offering circulates exhaustion.

There is a precise moment when offering crosses a line: it happens when giving becomes bargaining. If I do this, they will finally see me. If I give enough, I will be safe. Once giving becomes bargaining, the offering is no longer a gift. It is a bid. And bids do not have gates—they escalate.

THE GOD IN OFFERING

At Lughnasadh, the first harvest arrives. The God offers himself to the land—not because the land demanded it endlessly, but because the season was ripe. The grain is cut. What grew must now be given. Labor becomes sustenance. The offering is real, and it costs something real.

But notice what makes this offering sacred rather than destructive: it comes from what has matured. The God does not offer from the seed. He offers from the harvest—from what has had time to form, to ripen, to reach fullness. And the offering has a gate. He gives, and then he begins his descent. The giving does not continue indefinitely. It is consecrated to a season, not to an endless demand.

This is the image that modern burnout most desperately needs. We live in a world that demands Lughnasadh every day—perpetual harvest, perpetual cutting, perpetual giving—without ever allowing the field to lie fallow. The God's offering at Lughnasadh teaches that sacred giving is bounded. It arrives in its season. It is given from ripeness, not from desperation. And it ends.

If your giving has no gate, no season, no end—if you are harvesting from a field that has not been allowed to rest—then what you are doing, however noble it feels, is not the God's offering. It is extraction wearing sacred clothing.

What Lughnasadh reveals, however, is that sacred offering does not end with the act of giving. It alters the one who gives.

When the harvest is cut, the field is no longer what it was. What stood upright now lies in sheaves. What was green now dries. The act of offering changes the form of what has grown. It converts vitality into sustenance.

The God's offering marks this irreversible crossing.

He enters a transformation that the harvest demands. He has given, and that giving has changed him. Modern time resists this threshold. It demands bread without permitting the field to lie empty.

But the God himself does not remain in offering forever.

He gives.

And then he turns.

That turning is not failure.

It is the beginning of Return.

RETURN

Return is the season modern life treats as failure. Not always out loud. Often subtly—through the way it rewards availability, glorifies endurance, and frames withdrawal as laziness. In collapsed time, Return is tolerated only as emergency: when you are sick enough, broken enough, or depleted enough to justify stopping.

But in the God's arc, Return is not emergency. It is sacred order. The God offers, and then he disappears. Not as defeat. As completion.

Return includes concealment—letting something remain unseen without panicking. Fallow—allowing a field to stop producing so soil can recover. Disappearance—stepping back from the roles and commitments that have consumed you. Reduced demand.

Reconstitution. Rebuilding strength, coherence, and inward contact.

Most people do not resist Return because they hate rest. They resist Return because Return threatens something that has been keeping them safe. Return can feel like falling behind, losing relevance, losing approval, losing identity, or inviting criticism. In collapsed time, identity often becomes fused with output: I am what I accomplish. Return dissolves this fusion.

This is why Return is not merely physical. It is spiritual. It is the dismantling of a false theology—the theology that says your worth must be continuously proven.

THE GOD IN RETURN

At Samhain, the God relinquishes form. He has risen, reigned, offered, and now he descends. The veil thins. Authority is released. Life withdraws into memory and seed. The visible God becomes invisible—not destroyed, but concealed. He enters the dark not as defeat, but as completion of the arc.

This is the image our culture cannot tolerate: the voluntary disappearance of what was powerful. We understand loss. We understand failure. We understand being forced out. But voluntary descent—stepping back from visibility, from relevance, from productivity, because the season requires it—this feels like death to a world that equates existence with output.

And yet the world does not end when the God descends. The Wheel turns. Yule follows Samhain.

The light returns. Renewal becomes possible precisely because withdrawal occurred. The God who refused to descend—who clung to the crown, who kept offering past the gate, who would not let himself be unseen—that God would break the Wheel. The arc would become a straight line. And straight lines do not renew.

If you are afraid that stepping back means disappearing forever—that if you stop being visible, productive, available, you will cease to matter—the God's descent at Samhain offers a different promise: what descends returns. What rests renews. What disappears into the dark is not gone. It is gathering the conditions for its next becoming.

A field left fallow is not failing. It is recovering fertility—rebuilding the unseen conditions that make future harvest possible.

And the most important distinction: collapse is Return forced by depletion. Return is withdrawal chosen in its proper season. The aim is not to avoid hard seasons. The aim is to stop requiring catastrophe to justify restoration.

But there is a second distinction that must be named with equal care: Return is not the same as avoidance. Return restores capacity. Avoidance protects against feeling. Return is quiet but alive—you can sense something rebuilding, even slowly.

Avoidance is numb. Return eventually produces renewed readiness, even if modest. Avoidance produces nothing but the need for more avoidance.

If your withdrawal has lasted a long time and you feel no stirring of capacity, no gradual rebuilding, no quiet sense of something forming—if concealment feels less like restoration and more like disappearance from yourself—that may not be Return. That may be depression, dissociation, or grief that has not yet found support. The Wheel does not ask you to diagnose yourself. But it does ask you to be honest: sacred concealment should eventually produce something. If it produces only numbness, the season may need more than the Wheel can offer, and seeking professional support is not a failure of the framework. It is fidelity to the truth the framework is built on.

Return, in its true form, does not erase what came before. It preserves it differently.

Nothing the God became is lost. His authority does not vanish. His offering does not unravel. What he has been remains, but no longer in visible form. It passes into structure rather than display. It becomes inheritance rather than activity.

This is why the descent must happen before Becoming can begin again.

The God does not return to the beginning unchanged. He returns carrying memory.

What descends into concealment carries forward what it has learned. The next cycle does not repeat the last one identically. It unfolds from what has been integrated.

Return, therefore, is not regression. It is consolidation.

The modern world fears this phase because it cannot measure it. There is nothing to show. Nothing to optimize. Nothing to accelerate. Return removes you from the economy of proof.

And yet without it, nothing remains trustworthy.

Power that never relinquishes itself becomes brittle. Offering that never ends becomes depletion.

Authority that never steps down becomes tyranny. Becoming that never rests becomes fragmentation.

Return restores proportion.

It releases you from the illusion that your continuity depends on your visibility.

Winter closes.

The crown is set down.

The field lies fallow.

And beneath what appears empty, the next arc quietly prepares itself.

The Wheel does not break.

It turns.

• • •

REFLECTION

Which of the four seasons feels most natural to you? Which feels most illegitimate?

Where are you substituting performance for stability—proving, rushing, overfunctioning?

Which of your current offerings feel chosen and ripe, and which feel pressured or endless?

Where have you been treating Return as failure, laziness, or something you must earn?

What fear arises when you imagine stepping back—losing approval, falling behind, losing identity?

CHAPTER 3

MANY WHEELS AT ONCE

One of the first objections a reader is likely to raise is this: "But my life isn't one thing. I have work, children, a marriage, a household, a body, and a dozen moving parts. Surely they can't all be in the same season."

They can't. And they don't need to be.

The Wheel of the Year is not a single season you must impose across your entire life. It is a pattern of timing that applies per domain—and then a second principle that governs how those domains relate to one another.

A career may be in Offering while the body is in Return. Parenting may be in Authority while a creative life is still in Becoming. A relationship may be in Repair while spiritual life is asking for Withdrawal. This is not a flaw in the system. It is the actual shape of adult life.

Burnout tends to arrive not because you have multiple domains—everyone does—but because too many domains are forced into expansion at the same time, while Return is removed from the system entirely.

EXPANSION AND PRESERVATION

Before we go further, a distinction must be made clear, because it changes how the entire Wheel applies to real adult life.

A domain is in Offering mode—what we might more precisely call expansion mode—when it requires surplus energy, initiation, creative generation, emotional output beyond maintenance, growth, or visibility. A domain is in Authority mode—preservation mode—when it requires stewardship, governance, maintenance, clear boundaries, protection of continuity, and containment of demand.

This is not about activity versus inactivity.

Preservation is not passive. A marriage in Authority is not a dead marriage. A parent in Authority is not a negligent parent. A job in Authority is not a failing career. Preservation is the mode that keeps what already exists alive and stable so that it can endure the season.

Expansion grows. Preservation protects. Both are forms of devotion. But they draw on different reserves—and that difference is the key to surviving real adult life without burning out.

THE EXPANSION PRINCIPLE

The original version of this principle was stated as a hard cap: no more than two domains in Offering at any time. But real adult life revealed that this phrasing, while directionally true, could sound like a rule handed down from a monastery. Parenting does not rotate off. Jobs do not pause. Marriage does not disappear.

So the principle is stated more precisely here:

In any given season, expansion must be selective. If more than two domains require surplus energy at once, something will erode.

This is not a moral instruction. It is a statement about what finite systems can sustain. You can run three or four domains in expansion mode for a while—many people do, for months or even years—but the cost accumulates. It is paid in sleep, in health, in relational erosion, in spiritual dryness, in the slow narrowing of your inner life until the only thing left is output.

The principle does not ask you to abandon your responsibilities. It asks you to be honest about which of your responsibilities currently require expansion energy and which can be shifted into preservation mode without being abandoned.

THE DIFFERENCE BETWEEN OFFERING AND AUTHORITY IN MARRIAGE

This is where the Wheel must prove itself against the most common objection: a married person with children and a career is already in perpetual offering mode in three areas. Telling them to reduce to two can sound dismissive at best, cruel at worst. So what does it actually mean to run a partnership as Authority rather than Offering? It does not mean withholding affection, becoming emotionally distant, treating the relationship like a business contract, or reducing romance to zero. It means shifting the mode of the relationship during high-demand seasons.

A marriage in Offering mode looks like expansion: generative emotional output, long-form processing, deep conversations about growth, romantic initiation, creative intimacy, shared adventures, the building of something new together. This is beautiful. It is also expensive—it requires emotional surplus.

A marriage in Authority mode looks like preservation: clear check-ins instead of constant processing.

Shared decisions instead of emotional improvisation. Explicit agreements instead of vague expectations. Protecting sleep and logistics before protecting date-night aesthetics.

Reducing unnecessary relational negotiations. Authority in partnership says: *We are not here to generate romance right now. We are here to preserve the bond.*

That preservation may include fewer fights because you pre-decide policies, fewer misunderstandings because expectations are clarified, fewer resentments because labor is named. Authority protects continuity. Offering expands. In crisis seasons, preservation must precede expansion.

This matters for burnout because if work and parenting are already in Offering mode—both demanding outward energy—and the marriage is also required to be in Offering mode—constant emotional output, constant romantic generation—the adult is living in triple expansion. There is no governance. There is no containment. There is no descent. Authority in partnership reduces extraction. It might sound like: "We are in a two-year grind season. Let's agree to simplify." Or: "We will not interpret fatigue as rejection." Or: "We will protect each other's return time."

Authority is not cold. It is mature. It prevents the relationship from becoming another site of premature sacrifice.

And romance? Romance is Offering. Offering returns when capacity returns. The God is not crowned and sacrificed at the same time. He rises, reigns, offers, descends. Marriage follows a similar rhythm. There are seasons of expansion. There are seasons of governance. There are seasons of restoration. There are seasons of celebration. The problem is not that marriage shifts modes. The problem is expecting it to remain in peak Offering indefinitely.

The Difference Between Offering and Authority in Parenting

Parenting presents its own version of this challenge, because parenting never fully leaves your life the way a project or a job might. The children are there. The needs are real. The demand is ongoing. But parenting, like marriage, can shift between expansion and preservation.

Parenting in Offering mode looks like new developmental pushes, intensive enrichment, emotional deep dives with your children, constant availability, and building new structures for a new stage.

Parenting in Authority mode looks like routines, clear boundaries, fewer extracurricular activities, stability over stimulation, and protection of the household rhythm rather than expansion of it.

Both are loving. One expands. One preserves.

A parent who shifts into Authority mode during a heavy work season is not neglecting their children. They are governing the household so the family can survive the season intact. They are choosing consistency over novelty, steadiness over enrichment, structure over spontaneity. This is not a lesser form of parenting. It is parenting that knows what season it is in.

The injury happens when parents believe they must be in expansion mode at all times—constantly providing new experiences, constantly processing emotions at depth, constantly available for every developmental moment while also advancing a career and sustaining a marriage. That is not devoted parenting. It is a triple offering with no gate. And it will, eventually, produce the very instability it was trying to prevent.

A Household with Four Rooms

Imagine your life as a small household with four rooms. In one room, the fire is tended, and the meals are served—Offering. In another, the doors are locked, and the supplies are counted—Authority. In a third, something is quietly forming under cloth—Becoming. In the last room, the lights are dim, and the body sleeps—Return.

A household becomes strained when every room is turned into a kitchen, serving endlessly. Or when every room is turned into a control room, endlessly managing. Or when the room of Return is boarded up because it feels indulgent.

The aim is not to make all rooms do the same thing. The aim is to keep the household turning in season.

SCENARIO: YOUNG CHILDREN AND A STABLE JOB

Parenting is in Authority—protect sleep, maintain routines, reduce optional enrichment, and simplify expectations.

Marriage is in Authority—clear check-ins, fewer emotional marathons, shared logistics, and protect each other's rest.

Work is in Offering—career growth, initiative, and expansion.

Here, only one domain is in expansion. Everything else is governed. This is sustainable.

SCENARIO: CAREER SURGE AND AN AGING PARENT

Work is in Offering. Parent caregiving is in Offering—a temporary surge that demands real surplus energy.

Marriage shifts to Authority.

Parenting of one's own children shifts to Authority.

Two domains are in expansion. All others must stabilize, not expand. Romance becomes lighter. Household expectations simplify. Friendships may pause.

This is triage, not failure.

SCENARIO: A RELATIONSHIP RENEWAL SEASON

The children are older. Work is steady. Marriage moves into Offering—retreat, depth conversations, shared projects, creative intimacy.

Work and parenting shift into Authority.

The surplus that was once consumed by career or childcare is now intentionally directed toward the bond. This is what expansion looks like when it is chosen rather than extracted.

SCENARIO: THE SINGLE PARENT

Everything said so far assumes that a partner exists to share governance. For a single parent, that assumption does not hold. There is no one to shift the partnership into Authority with. There is no second adult to absorb the logistics, the emotional labor, the nighttime waking, the decision fatigue.

The single parent carries what a household of two would share—and carries it alone.

This is not a theoretical hardship. It is a structural reality that changes how the Wheel must be applied.

For a single parent, the expansion principle is even more critical because the margin is thinner. If work is the primary Offering—and it often must be, because income is survival—then parenting must be governed, not expanded. This does not mean parenting less. It means parenting with maximum structure and minimum improvisation: clear routines, predictable rhythms, fewer optional commitments, simpler meals, and a household run on consistency rather than constant reinvention.

Authority parenting for a single parent is not a compromise. It is a survival architecture that protects the parent's capacity to continue showing up.

The single parent operates without a relational buffer — and this is worth naming clearly, not as a deficiency but as a structural reality that shapes how the Wheel applies. In a two-parent household, one partner's collapse can be temporarily absorbed by the other. A single parent's architecture does not include this redundancy. The structure is leaner, which means it must also be more intentional.

This means that Return is not merely important — it is non-negotiable, and it must often be built from smaller, more protected increments. Ten minutes of concealment after the children are in bed. A firm boundary around one evening a week. A simplified weekend that does not require performative output. The Wheel does not pretend this is easy.

What it can do is refuse to add guilt to an already intentional life. The single parent who governs the household, maintains the job, and protects even a sliver of Return is not failing to offer enough. They are keeping the arc alive inside a structure they have built and are holding — and that deserves to be named for what it is: devotion made architectural.

If you are a single parent and this book has felt as though it was written for someone with more margin than you have, know this: the principle is the same, but the scale is different. Your gates may be smaller. Your Return may be briefer. Your Authority may need to cover more ground. None of that diminishes the Wheel's relevance to your life. If anything, the Wheel's insistence that you deserve seasons — that even a tightly held life is not meant to be perpetual Offering — may matter more for you than for anyone.

FRIENDSHIP, COMMUNITY, AND THE INVISIBLE OFFERING

There is one domain the book has not yet named that many burned-out people carry without recognizing it: social and community obligation. Friendships, extended family relationships, volunteer commitments, neighborhood networks, spiritual communities—these are often treated as though they exist outside the economy of offering. They do not. Maintaining friendships requires emotional output. Volunteering requires time and energy. Community roles—the person who organizes, the person who remembers birthdays, the person who checks in—require sustained attention that is rarely named as labor but always costs something.

Like every other domain, social life can expand or be preserved.

Friendship in Offering mode looks like deep emotional processing, initiating plans, showing up for every crisis, and building new relationships.

Friendship in Authority mode looks like maintaining connection through simple gestures—a brief text, a standing monthly dinner, the honest words: "I am in a heavy season. I am not disappearing. I just have less to give right now."

Many people—especially those who have been trained to equate goodness with availability—will resist shifting friendships into Authority mode. It feels like abandonment. It feels like selfishness. But a friendship that requires you to expend an emotional surplus you do not have is a friendship operating in extraction, not in love. True friendship can survive a season of governance. If it cannot, the relationship was drawing on your premature sacrifice rather than on a genuine connection.

THE CORE INSIGHT

The problem is not that adults have multiple responsibilities. The problem is when every domain demands growth at once—emotional overfunctioning, constant relational output, career striving, parenting expansion, social maintenance, spiritual growth—all in Offering mode. No gates. No Authority. No containment.

Not everything in your life can be in expansion at the same time. That is clean, true, and non-moralizing.

The Wheel does not ask you to make everything even. Life is rarely even. The aim is simpler and more sacred: offer only where offering is in season and ripe. Govern what must be sustained. Protect what is forming. Return where return is needed.

• • •

REFLECTION

What are your four to six primary domains right now?

Which domains are currently in expansion—requiring surplus energy, growth, or initiative—whether you admit it or not?

Where have you been demanding expansion from a domain that could survive in preservation mode?

What would Authority look like there?

If your marriage or partnership is currently in Authority, can you name that honestly—and can you see it as mature rather than diminished?

Which domain is asking for Return—and how have you been overruling it?

If you are parenting alone, where is the smallest gate you can protect—and what guilt do you need to release to protect it?

PART II

The Timing Wound

CHAPTER 4

THE BURNOUT THAT DOESN'T RESPOND TO REST

There is a kind of tiredness that sleep resolves. You work hard. You rest. Your body recovers. You return to your life intact. This is not the tiredness we are speaking of.

The burnout that concerns this book is the kind that lingers. It improves temporarily but reappears the moment you resume responsibility. You take a weekend off, and by Tuesday you feel as though you never rested. You take a vacation, and the exhaustion is waiting for you when you return. You reduce your workload, and yet something underneath remains strained.

You begin to suspect that the problem is you. Maybe you are less resilient than other people.

Maybe you are not disciplined enough. Maybe you are not built for the life you have.

But what if the problem is not weakness? What if the problem is timing?

YOU MIGHT RECOGNIZE THIS

She is a therapist who cries in her car between sessions but tells herself that's just the cost of caring. She sleeps well, exercises, eats properly. She has read every burnout book on the shelf. Nothing reaches the thing underneath. She suspects she is simply not suited for the work she loves, when in truth, she has been in Offering for seven years without a single gate.

He is a father of three who works a stable job and coaches Little League on weekends. He has not had an unpressured evening in two years. When his wife suggests a weekend away, he feels panic instead of relief—because he cannot imagine who will hold everything together. He is not overworked by any single measure. He is over-crowned: carrying Authority in every domain with no Return in sight.

She is a community organizer who built a mutual aid network during the pandemic and has not been able to step back since. Every boundary she sets triggers guilt. She equates her exhaustion with proof that the work matters. She is not selfish. She is in premature sacrifice—offering from a place that ran out of harvest two years ago.

None of these people are broken. All of them are living in the wrong season.

Ordinary Fatigue and Structural Exhaustion

Ordinary fatigue follows exertion. It has a clear cause. It responds to restoration. It resolves when demand decreases.

Structural exhaustion does not behave this way. It persists because it is not merely a depletion of energy. It is a depletion of continuity—the sense that your effort exists within a larger pattern that includes completion, descent, and renewal. When continuity is intact, exertion feels costly but meaningful. When continuity is broken, exertion feels endless.

Structural exhaustion feels like being responsible without a threshold, giving without a visible end, carrying without governance, performing without interruption, and remaining visible without concealment.

You may not be working more hours than before. What has changed is not quantity. It is that something in your life no longer turns.

THE ILLUSION OF RECOVERY

When burnout does not respond to rest, we assume the rest was insufficient. So we try again. We sleep more. We cancel more. We retreat more. But if the structure remains unchanged, rest becomes interruption rather than renewal.

You pause. Then you re-enter the same configuration of demand: the same open loops, the same expectation of availability, and the same absence of closure. Nothing in the architecture has shifted. So the exhaustion returns—because rest alone cannot repair misalignment.

Imagine a field that is never allowed to lie fallow. You could water it, fertilize it, and tend it carefully. But if harvest is demanded continuously, depletion is inevitable.

THE HIDDEN MORAL INJURY

There is another layer to this exhaustion. It is not only physical strain. It is moral strain. You begin to feel that you are failing at something essential: failing to keep up, failing to be dependable, failing to be strong enough to carry what you once could.

This is the cruelty of structural burnout. It disguises a timing injury as a personal deficiency. If you are living in a season of perpetual output—perpetual Authority or perpetual Offering—your system will eventually destabilize. Not because you are weak, but because no living system can remain in those conditions indefinitely.

WHEN LIFE STOPS TURNING

Burnout that does not respond to rest usually shares one feature: life feels like one long stretch of the same demand. You are always reachable. Always responsible. Always slightly behind. Always slightly braced. Even when you rest, the structure does not close. There are no gates.

Without gates, exertion is never complete. Without completion, renewal never arrives. This is why you can sleep eight hours and wake up already tired. This is why your nervous system remains activated even in stillness. Your body is not asking for more rest. It is asking for rhythm.

A Different Diagnosis

This book proposes a different diagnosis. Burnout is often not the result of too much effort alone. It is the result of remaining in one mode of effort without the counterbalance that preserves continuity.

If you are perpetually giving, something in you must eventually descend. If you are perpetually stabilizing, something in you must eventually withdraw. If you are perpetually visible, something in you must eventually disappear. This is not a weakness. It is the rhythm beneath all living things.

If rest has not restored you, consider this possibility: you may not be broken. Your life may simply have stopped turning.

Reflection

When you rest, does the exhaustion resolve—or does it return the moment you resume your responsibilities?

Where in your life does demand feel unbounded or without threshold? When was the last time something truly ended for you?

Do you feel more in need of sleep—or more in need of closure?

What would it mean to consider your exhaustion a signal of misalignment rather than a personal failure?

CHAPTER 5

The Collapse of Sacred Time

We have named the exhaustion. Now we name what created it. There is a particular kind of fatigue that cannot be solved by better habits. It is not the tiredness that follows honest labor or the exhaustion of a difficult season. It is the wear that comes from living inside a world that no longer honors *when*.

In such a world, time is treated as an unbroken surface: an endless day lit by artificial light and governed by notifications, demand, and throughput. There is no dusk that truly closes anything. There is no winter that is allowed to be winter. There is no time for the field to lie fallow. There is only the expectation of continuity—produce, respond, prove   regardless of season, capacity, or consequence.

This is what I mean by the collapse of sacred time.

Sacred time is not "spiritual time" in the decorative sense. It is the recognition that life moves through recognizable conditions—that there is an order to ripening, that there are gates between phases, and that the gates matter. A field is not harvested in spring. A seed is not judged by its lack of fruit. A body is not asked to grieve and perform at the same time. In living systems, timing is not an optional accessory. It is a functional necessity.

The World Without Gates

Most traditional cosmologies—especially those rooted in land, season, and agriculture—assume that time is not uniform. It has texture. It changes its demands. There are seasons where you must act, and seasons where action is wrong.

Modern life has not simply lost touch with this. It has built systems that actively oppose it. Digital time is always available. Work time leaks into home time.

Home time leaks into sleep. Consumption fills the pauses that used to signal endings. Even spiritual practices are often folded into the same logic: content, output, consistency, results.

The result is that the gates between seasons are removed. Without gates, you can no longer feel the difference between labor and offering, urgency and readiness, responsibility and extraction, devotion and compulsion, return and avoidance. Everything becomes one blended category: demand.

And when demand becomes the only season, the body has only two options: comply or collapse. Many people do both—they comply until they collapse and recover just enough to comply again.

THE UNSPOKEN THEOLOGY OF MODERN TIME

Every culture has a theology of time, even when it does not call it theology. It answers questions like: What counts as a good day? What is a life for? What is acceptable to stop? Who is allowed to rest—and under what conditions?

Modern time carries an unspoken theology so pervasive it can feel like reality itself:

• Continuity is virtue—keep going, keep producing, keep responding.

• Visibility is proof—if you are not seen, you are not real.

• Speed is competence.

• Rest must be justified—earned, optimized, or medically necessary.

• Everything can be improved—even the parts of life that require rest.

This theology doesn't simply pressure you. It trains your nervous system. It teaches you that stopping is suspicious, that slowness is failure, that withdrawal is avoidance, that quiet peace is laziness, and that limits are selfish.

WHEN DEVOTION BECOMES DEPLETION

This matters especially for spiritually serious people. When sacred time collapses, the hunger for meaning does not disappear—it intensifies. Many people respond to the pressure of modern times by reaching for spiritual language as a way to make their endurance feel purposeful. Meaning can hold a person through hardship. But collapsed time creates a subtle danger: spiritual seriousness can become one more way you comply with extraction.

Many exhausted people are not exhausted because they are selfish or chaotic. They are exhausted because they are conscientious. They keep promises. They show up. They notice what needs doing. They carry responsibility without needing applause. In a collapsed time economy, these traits become exploitable.

The world will always find a way to convert conscience into fuel. A workplace will reward the person who stays late and answers fastest. A family system will lean on the one who keeps things together. A community will expect the most reliable person to become a constant volunteer. And the person who is spiritually serious—who believes in meaning, who values responsibility, who wants to live with integrity, often becomes the easiest to extract from, because they do not want to be the kind of person who refuses.

Over time, goodness becomes availability. Depletion begins to feel like proof. If you are tired, you must be giving. If you are giving, you must be good. If you stop giving, you must be failing.

This is not devotion. It is a moral trap.

THE HIDDEN BARGAIN

Depletion often contains a bargain—usually unspoken, sometimes unconscious: if I give enough, I will be safe. If I give enough, I will be loved. If I give enough, I will be indispensable. If I give enough, I can outrun guilt.

This bargain can come from family systems, religious formation, trauma, or simply years of being praised for being the one who can handle it. However it forms, it has the same effect: you begin to offer not from ripeness, but from anxiety. Your giving becomes strategic—not in a malicious way, but often in a desperate one. The nervous system learns that giving is how you maintain connection, stability, and belonging.

But the Wheel refuses to sanctify this. The Wheel asks that offerings be rightly timed. Return is part of devotion, not the absence of it.

A necessary pause: if you recognized yourself in the bargain just described, you may feel a flush of shame—as though discovering the anxiety beneath your giving means your giving was fake, manipulative, or worthless. It was not. The bargain is almost always formed in childhood, in crisis, or in systems that taught you that love must be earned through performance. It is not a character flaw. It is a survival strategy that once kept you safe and connected. Naming it is not an accusation. It is the beginning of giving from a freer place. The goal is not to be ashamed of how you learned to love. The goal is to let love become less expensive.

RETURN AS DEVOTION

Return is not the absence of devotion. It reestablishes the conditions that make true devotion possible. Return is how you honor the fact that you are a living system, not an infinite resource.

For many people, reclaiming Return will not feel holy at first. It will feel like guilt. It will feel like selfishness. It will feel like letting someone down.

This is one of the clearest signs that devotion has been miscast as depletion: when the act of returning feels like moral failure.

If that is true for you, do not rush to correct the feeling. Notice it. Let it reveal what has been trained into you.

REFLECTION

Where does your life currently have no gates—no true ending to the day, the work, the caretaking, or the demand?

What have you been trained to treat as lazy or selfish that might actually be right?

Where do you equate urgency with importance, or speed with worth?

Where have you begun to equate being good with being endlessly available?

What do you fear would happen—relationally, materially, spiritually—if you reduced your giving?

CHAPTER 6

PREMATURE SACRIFICE

Now we give the pattern its proper name.

Premature sacrifice is offering what has not reached readiness. It is giving from the seed rather than from the harvest. It is consecrating what is still forming. It is spending what your life has not yet earned. It is pouring out from a place that needs protection, then calling the emptiness virtue.

Premature sacrifice is one of the most common spiritual injuries of modern life because it is structured to demand continuous offerings. It does not care whether you are ripe. It cares whether you are available.

THE MISTAKE WE CALL NOBILITY

Premature sacrifice often arrives wearing noble clothing. You do not wake up and decide to destroy yourself. You decide to be responsible. You decide to show up. You decide to be the kind of person who can handle it.

And then—quietly—something shifts. You begin to offer not from capacity, but from fear. Not from ripeness, but from urgency. Not by choice, but under pressure. Your giving becomes early.

Early looks like committing before you have the bandwidth, saying yes because you cannot bear the guilt of no, producing work before it is formed because visibility feels like survival, giving emotionally when you are already depleted because you think love requires it, turning rest into a reward you must earn—then never earning it.

The danger is that premature sacrifice does not feel like a mistake. It feels like character. It feels like faithfulness. It feels like being a good person in a difficult world.

What Readiness Actually Means

Readiness is not enthusiasm. It is not pressure. It is not urgency. Readiness is viability.

A thing is ready to be offered when offering it does not damage the conditions that allow you to continue living. This includes the body—sleep, health, nervous system stability. The household—money, time, logistics, relational repair capacity.

The soul—meaning, inner life, quiet, desire that is not coerced. And the future—space for Return, space for Becoming, space for renewal.

Premature sacrifice happens when you offer at the cost of these conditions, especially when the offering becomes recursive — when you begin to offer habitually from a place that is already starving.

The Two Tests

If you remember nothing else from this chapter, remember these two tests. They will clarify almost everything.

Test One: Does this offering leave me intact? Not comfortable. Not untouched. Intact. If the offering predictably erodes sleep, health, stability, or relational capacity, it is either mistimed or overextended—no matter how meaningful it feels.

Test Two: Is there a gate? Does the offering have an end? Is there closure? Is there a Return planned, protected, and real? If there is no gate, it is not a sacred offering. It is an open drain.

These tests are not meant to shame you. They are meant to protect you from spiritualizing what is actually extraction.

THE TESTS IN PRACTICE

Your sister asks you to host the family holiday gathering. You love your family. You want to say yes. But you have been in a caregiving season for six months, your house is in disrepair, and you are already behind on sleep.

Test One: Does hosting leave you intact? Honest answer: no. It will cost you a week of recovery you do not have.

Test Two: Is there a gate? There could be—if you set a clear end time and ask others to share the labor.

The repair: Say yes to a simplified version with a hard stop at 7 pm, or say "not this year" and let the grief be real without letting it override the truth.

Your manager offers you a high-visibility project. It would be excellent for your career. But you are also navigating a difficult season in your marriage, and your sleep has been fractured for weeks.

Test One: Does taking this project leave you intact?

Probably not—two domains are already in expansion.

Test Two: Is there a gate? The project has a deadline, so yes.

The repair is not necessarily to decline, but to be honest about what must shift into preservation if you accept: the marriage moves into Authority mode, social obligations reduce, and you install a hard return gate after the project ends.

A close friend calls in distress and wants to process for an hour. You care about her deeply. But you are already depleted—you gave it all emotionally at work, and you have nothing left.

Test One: Does this leave you intact? Not tonight.

Test Two: Is there a gate? Not unless you make one.

The repair: "I love you, and I want to hear this. Can we talk Thursday evening when I can actually be present? Tonight, I would be giving you an empty version of myself." That is not rejection. It is timing.

How to Stop Offering Early

Stopping premature sacrifice begins with small restorations of timing.

Delay one offering. Choose one thing you habitually give—time, emotional labor, responsiveness, extra work—and delay it. Not forever. Just long enough to restore the sense that giving has timing.

Add a gate. Give something a clear beginning and end. "I can do this for 30 minutes." "I can help with this today, but not all week." Gates protect offering from becoming endless.

Protect what is still forming. Name one domain that is in Becoming—your health, your creativity, your relationship with yourself—and stop demanding harvest from it. Treat it as seed. Seeds do not prove themselves. They are protected until they are viable.

Premature sacrifice ends when you stop confusing early giving with virtue and start honoring viability as sacred.

Reflection

Where are you offering from what is not yet ready—time, energy, emotional labor, money, creativity, attention?

What do you fear would happen if you delayed that offering?

Which of your current offerings have a clear gate, and which are open drains?

Where are you confusing early giving with goodness, faithfulness, or devotion?

What is one small repair you can make this week: delay one offering, add one gate, or protect one seed?

PART III

LIVING THE WHEEL

CHAPTER 7

FINDING YOUR CURRENT SEASON

The Wheel becomes most dangerous when it becomes an identity. People learn the language—Becoming, Authority, Offering, Return—and then use it to judge themselves. They decide which season is good, which season is bad, and they try to force themselves into the season that seems most acceptable.

That is not living the Wheel. That is collapsed time wearing sacred vocabulary.

To live the Wheel is to tell the truth about the season you are already in—then stop acting as if you are somewhere else.

SEASONS ARE CONDITIONS, NOT MOODS

A season is not a feeling. It is a condition that has requirements. You may feel energized and still be in Return, because the nervous system is finally letting go. You may feel sad and still be in Offering, because the work is ripe even if you are tender. You may feel restless and still be in Becoming, because you want proof.

So we do not locate your season by asking how you feel. We locate your season by asking what life requires right now for viability.

THE SEASON QUESTIONS

Becoming: What is forming that must be protected? Where is life re-organizing beneath the surface? What is tender, incomplete, or still gathering structure?

Where would forcing clarity or output cause distortion? The correct posture is restraint.

Authority: What must be governed to preserve continuity? What needs limits, structure, or containment? Where am I overfunctioning instead of governing? The correct posture is governance.

Offering: What is ripe to be given with a gate? What is ready to be delivered, released, or completed?

Where must I end it to keep it holy? The correct posture is consecrated release.

Return: What must withdraw for renewal to occur? Where is the system asking to reduce demand? What has been over-extracted and must be restored? The correct posture is withdrawal.

You do not need perfect answers. The season that makes you slightly uncomfortable is often the true one.

THREE COMMON MISREADS

Mistaking anxiety for Offering. Many people assume urgency means readiness. They feel pressure and interpret it as "I must act now." But urgency is not ripeness. If acting now would require you to sacrifice sleep, stability, or sanity, you are likely not in ripe Offering.

Mistaking control for Authority. Some people respond to overwhelm by tightening everything: more rules, more tracking, more perfection. This feels like governance, but it is often fear. True Authority reduces cost. If your structure increases panic and rigidity, you are not governing—you are bracing.

Mistaking collapse for Return. People wait until they break, then call it Return. But collapse is not true Return; it is Return forced by depletion. Return begins earlier. Return is chosen.

THE WEEKLY LEDGER

Once a week, take ten minutes and write this:

Global season: Becoming, Authority, Offering, or Return.

Then list four to six domains. For each, write the season, the current demand in one sentence, the right posture (protect, govern, offer, or withdraw), and one repair (one gate, one delay, one simplification, one return pocket).

The goal is not to fix your life in one sitting. The goal is to stop acting blindly from a season that is not yours.

STOP ACTING AS IF

Once you locate your season, the Wheel asks for one act of integrity: stop acting as if you are in a different season.

If you are in Return, stop making new offerings. If you are in Becoming, stop demanding proof.

If you are in Authority, stop overfunctioning and choose a limit.

If you are in Offering, stop bargaining and add a gate.

You may not be able to change everything. But you can stop committing the specific violation that keeps the wound open.

That is integrity in the Wheel.

Not perfect alignment.

Not a flawless year.

One act of truth: naming where you are, and refusing to live as if you are somewhere else.

The season turns when you stop violating it.

The arc resumes.

CHAPTER 8

REPAIRING THE TIMELINE

Finding your current season gives you truth.

Repairing the timeline gives you a way to act on that truth without fantasy.

Most people are not burned out because they don't understand rhythm. They are burned out because they are living inside constraints that continually push them out of season. They know they need Return, but life keeps demanding Offering. They sense Becoming, but money demands harvest.

The question becomes practical: what do you do when the season you are in is not the season your life is demanding?

REPAIR IS NOT BALANCE

Repair means stop the hemorrhage. It means restore enough timing that your system can remain viable. It means protect Return where you can, protect Becoming where you must, and refuse premature sacrifice wherever it is costing you your future.

In constrained seasons, repair is often modest. But modest repair done consistently has more power than dramatic plans you cannot sustain.

WHEN YOU ARE IN PREMATURE SACRIFICE

You know you are in premature sacrifice when you keep giving while your body is asking for Return; your giving has no gate, you feel morally trapped, and resentment is present but overridden by "should."

Name the unripe offering. Do not name ten things. Name one. Write a sentence: "I am offering this from a place that is not ready to give."

Add a gate immediately. "I can do this until 7 pm." "I can give 20 minutes." "I can respond tomorrow." If you cannot reduce the obligation itself, reduce the extraction around it: the overexplaining, the constant responsiveness, the perfectionism.

Convert one sacrifice into stewardship. Ask: What would it look like to give this without bleeding? Often, the answer is not to do less, but to do it differently—slower, with a boundary, with help, with a defined end.

Restore one Return pocket daily. Even ten minutes counts if it is real Return: no input, no demand, no proving.

WHEN YOU ARE LIVING IN URGENCY

Urgency is not the same as necessity. Necessity can be clean: This must be done. Urgency is chaotic: everything must be done now, and if it isn't, something bad will happen.

Separate "**due****"** from dread**. Write two columns: actually due (real deadlines, real consequences) and dread-driven (things you fear will happen if you slow down). Most people discover that dread is driving far more of their urgency than reality is.

Choose the next right thing. Urgency collapses time by making everything simultaneous. Repair restores sequence. What is the next right action that preserves continuity? Not the whole thing.

One action.

Install a "**not now****"** container.**** A single list, a note titled "After Friday." Putting something into "not now" is not avoidance. It is governance.

Practice deliberate slowness. Choose one routine action, do it 10% slower. This is not a mindfulness trick. It is nervous-system re-education: proof that time is not an emergency.

WHEN YOU ARE IN FORCED VISIBILITY

Forced visibility means you have lost concealment. You may not be posting online. You may still be in enforced visibility if you are constantly reachable, constantly monitored, constantly explaining yourself, constantly on emotionally, unable to be private without guilt.

Create one daily concealment window. Ten minutes is enough. No phone, no messages, no explaining, no output. You being unseen on purpose.

Stop pre-explaining. Choose one boundary and state it simply. No story. "I'm not available tonight." "I'll respond tomorrow." The point is not to be harsh. It is to stop offering beyond your limits.

Reduce one form of monitoring. Check email twice a day instead of twenty times. Turn off read receipts. Put the phone in another room after 8 p.m.

WHEN YOU CANNOT REDUCE DEMAND: WORKAROUNDS FOR CONSTRAINED LIVES

For the Caregiver Who Cannot Step Away If you are caring for someone with dementia, a newborn, a chronically ill family member, or a disabled dependent, you cannot install gates the way other chapters describe. The demand is not negotiable. The person in your care needs what they need.

The workaround is not to reduce care. It is to reduce everything around care. Eliminate every optional obligation. Lower household standards deliberately—not as failure, but as triage. Accept help without performing gratitude for it. Build micro-return into the cracks: five minutes in a locked bathroom with no purpose. One meal eaten sitting down. A nightly ritual that marks the end of your shift, even when the caregiving does not actually end. These are not luxuries. They are how you keep the arc turning inside a structure that does not allow it to turn fully.

For the Person in Financial Survival Mode When money is the primary pressure—when you are working two jobs, or when losing one day's pay means missing rent—the Wheel's counsel to "reduce your offerings" can sound like advice from another planet. The workaround here is not to pretend you have a margin you do not have. It is to refuse one thing: the addition of guilt to exhaustion. You are already carrying survival. Do not also carry the weight of believing you should be doing this differently.

Practical repair in financial precarity looks like this: one thing you will not add this week. Not one thing you will remove—one thing you will not take on. That is a gate. It is a small one. It is real.

Additionally, refuse to layer emotional labor on top of survival labor. If you are already working to keep the lights on, you do not also owe people your cheerfulness, your patience with their complaints, or your availability for their processing. Protect what little surplus you have from being converted into someone else's comfort.

For the Person Leaving a High-Control System If you were raised in—or spent years inside—a religious community, family system, or organization that demanded perpetual offerings as proof of loyalty, faith, or love, then your timeline wound has a specific shape. You were taught that rest is selfishness, that questioning is betrayal, that limits are evidence of weak devotion. The system's theology of time was itself the injury.

Repair here begins with a recognition that may feel disorienting: the exhaustion you feel is not because you failed the system. It is because the system was built on extraction and called it holiness. Your recovery may include grief—for the years given, for the sincerity that was exploited, for the version of devotion that you now see was not devotion at all. The Wheel does not ask you to rush that grief. It only asks you to stop carrying the old system's definition of what you owe.

A Repair Hierarchy

When you are out of season, repair in this order: first, restore Return somewhere, even micro-return. Second, add gates to offerings. Third, reduce forced visibility. Fourth, protect Becoming. Then build rhythm.

This hierarchy matters because rhythm is hard to build while you are hemorrhaging. Repair stops the bleed. Rhythm builds the future.

The Quiet Truth About Constraint

Sometimes you cannot fix the situation immediately. You cannot quit the job today. You cannot stop caregiving. You cannot remove the demand.

When that is true, repair is not about pretending you have freedom. Repair is about refusing to make the situation worse by committing additional violations. You may not be able to leave Offering—but you can add a gate. You may not be able to change the demand—but you can restore micro-return. You may not be able to stop—but you can stop proving.

This is what it means to repair the timeline: to bring pattern back into a constrained life so that the arc can turn again when conditions allow.

Reflection

Which violation is most active for you right now: premature sacrifice, urgency, or forced visibility?

What is one concrete gate you can add this week?

Where is dread driving urgency more than reality?

What is one small act of concealment you can protect daily without explanation?

CHAPTER 9

THE RHYTHM RULE

Repairing the timeline stops the hemorrhage. But a life can stop bleeding and still remain vulnerable—because the same conditions that pushed you out of season will push again.

So this chapter offers something simple on purpose: a rhythm rule. Not a perfect schedule. Not a self-optimization plan. A rhythm rule is a small set of gates that makes renewal structural, so you do not have to earn it through collapse.

A rule, in this sense, is not a punishment. It is a trellis: a structure that holds living things upright. It reduces decision fatigue. It preserves continuity. It protects Return before your body has to scream for it.

WHAT THE RHYTHM RULE PREVENTS

The rhythm rule exists to prevent three predictable failures: offering without gates—giving that never ends. Return as emergency—restoration only after collapse. Becoming treated as laziness—forcing harvest from seed.

If your rhythm rule prevents these three things, it is doing its job—even if everything else remains imperfect.

THE DAILY RULE: THREE GATES

Gate 1: The Start Gate. Collapsed time begins the moment you wake up and enter demand. The start gate is a brief act that places you back under the arc before urgency captures you. It can be one minute: feet on the floor, one slow breath. A sentence: "Today has gates." A question: "What season is my system in?" This is not a ritual for aesthetic comfort. It is a declaration: you are not entering the day as a resource to be extracted.

Gate 2: The Offering Gate. Most burnout is not caused by working or caring. It is caused by uncontained work and care. The offering gate defines the container: a hard stop time, a limit on responsiveness, a boundary around emotional labor, a defined work block with an end. Offering becomes holy when it has an end.

Gate 3: The Return Gate. The day must end. Not in theory—in practice. The return gate is the non-negotiable closure that tells your nervous system: you are released. Screens off at a certain hour. Phone out of the bedroom. Ten minutes of dim light and no input. If you build only one thing from this book, build a return gate.

THE WEEKLY RULE: A SABBATH OF SOME KIND

You do not need to call it Sabbath. You do not need to practice it in a religious way. But you do need a weekly rhythm that restores the arc.

The principle is simple: one day a week—or a protected slice of one—you do not exist primarily as output. In that time, the questions change: not "what should I accomplish?" but "what restores continuity?" If you cannot take a full day, take a slice. Sunday morning is quiet and unplanned. Friday night is sacred closure. Saturday afternoon is low-demand. What matters is that it is real, consistent, and protected.

THE SEASONAL RULE: ALTERNATING SEASONS OF OFFERING AND FALLOW

The Wheel is not only daily. It is seasonal. It contains expansion and contraction, visibility and concealment, harvest and fallow.

A simple seasonal rhythm:

• Two seasons of higher offerings.

• Two seasons of consolidation and authority.

• One season of deliberate fallow—less visibility, fewer new commitments, restoration.

Your actual seasons may not match the calendar perfectly. The point is not aesthetic alignment. The point is alternating modes, so the system is not extracted year-round. If you do not plan for fallow periods, they will arrive as collapse.

The Minimum Viable Rhythm Rule

If you are in constraint, here is the simplest version:

• One daily return gate of ten to twenty minutes, protected.

• One weekly low-demand block of two to four hours.

• One monthly "no new offerings" week or weekend.

This is enough to change a life because it changes the structure. It restores the principle that time has gates.

Three Rhythm Rules in Practice

Maria is a single mother of two who works full-time as a nurse. Her rhythm rule: phone goes in the drawer by 8:30 pm (return gate). Saturday mornings are unscheduled until noon (weekly return). She takes no new social commitments between September and December (seasonal fallow during the hardest work months). Her rule is modest. It has kept her functioning for two years.

David is a self-employed consultant with a partner and no children. His rhythm rule: he does not check email before 9 am or after 6 pm (start and offering gates). Sunday is a no-work day with no exceptions (weekly sabbath). He blocks one week after every major project delivery for recovery (seasonal return). When he breaks the rule—and he does, regularly—he restores it the next day without self--punishment.

Anika is a doctoral student caring for her aging mother while writing her dissertation. Her rhythm rule: she writes for no more than three hours per day (offering gate—she discovered that four hours produced diminishing returns and increasing anxiety). Tuesday evenings are hers alone (weekly return). She has told her advisor she will not take on new teaching in the spring semester (seasonal fallow). Her mother's care is governed by a shared schedule with her sister. When the schedule breaks down, she protects her Tuesday evening first—not because it is the most important thing, but because it is the gate that keeps everything else from collapsing.

Keeping It From Becoming Performance

The biggest risk is that you will turn rhythm into a new self-improvement project: perfect tracking, rigid rules, shame when you break them. So here is the instruction: the rhythm rule is not a test. It is a protection.

If you miss a gate, you do not punish yourself. You restore the next one. If a season becomes chaotic, you find the smallest place you can still make Return lawful. The purpose is continuity, not perfection.

Reflection

What is the smallest daily return gate you can protect for the next seven days—without negotiation?

Where does your day currently have no ending? What would be a lawful stop-time?

What form of weekly return is realistic for you right now?

If you planned one season of fallow time each year, what would you reduce?

CHAPTER 10

THE PERSONAL WHEEL PLAN

A rhythm rule gives you gates. A personal wheel plan gives you a year.

This is where the Wheel stops being an idea you love and becomes a structure your life can actually live inside. A personal wheel plan is the act of designing your commitments, offerings, rest, and thresholds so that you are no longer relying on collapse to force renewal.

CAPACITY IS SACRED

Most people build their year as if capacity is infinite. They build for ideals, for pressure, for fear, for other people's expectations. Then they try to survive through willpower. Then they collapse. Then they rebuild the same year again.

A personal wheel plan begins with a different assumption: capacity is sacred because it is finite. Not as limitation-as-shame. As limitation-as-law. The goal is not to fit everything in. The goal is to stop building a year that requires premature sacrifice.

STEP ONE: CHOOSE YOUR YEAR'S SHAPE

The Two-Harvest Year: Two major offering seasons, two consolidation seasons, one fallow season. Best for creators, entrepreneurs, project-based work.

The Caregiving Year: One primary offering domain that remains steady. Everything else arranged around governance and micro-return. Best for parents of young children, caregivers, people in medical seasons.

The Stewardship Year: Fewer launches, more maintenance. Deep authority season: boundaries, stability, continuity. Best for rebuilding after burnout, stabilizing finances, healing.

The Initiation Year: High Becoming: learning, training, reorientation. Limited public offering. Best for new directions, education, recovery, identity transitions.

Name your year's shape in one sentence. This sentence alone will prevent dozens of premature commitments.

STEP TWO: NAME YOUR PRIMARY DOMAINS

Choose the four to six domains that will define your year. Common domains: work or income, parenting or caregiving, body and health, home and logistics, relationship and community, creativity or calling or spiritual life.

Now ask: which domain is the primary offering domain this year? Most burnout comes from pretending there is no primary domain—pretending you can offer fully in every domain at once. Choose the truth.

STEP THREE: CHOOSE YOUR OFFERINGS

Choose what you will actually offer this year. Not what you might do. Not what you hope to do. No more than three true offerings for the year.

This is not because you are incapable of more. It is because an offering must have a gate and a Return. If you plan ten offerings, you are planning ten drains. If you feel grief here, let it be real. Most people are grieving the fantasy of infinite capacity. That grief is part of the Return you have been denied.

STEP FOUR: PLACE THE OFFERINGS INTO SEASONS

For each offering, assign a Becoming window (preparation and formation), an Authority window (governance and boundaries), an Offering window (delivery and release), and a Return window (recovery and fallow). The specific months matter less than the existence of the phases.

STEP FIVE: INSTALL THRESHOLDS

A threshold is a pre-decided stopping point that prevents your year from sliding into endless demand. Choose two or three thresholds: a maximum number of evenings per week you work. A "no new commitments" rule during certain seasons. A visibility threshold. A post-offering recovery period.

STEP SIX: SCHEDULE RETURN BEFORE YOU SCHEDULE MORE

Place Return into the year like it is non-negotiable. One fallow month, two recovery weeks scattered through the year, a quarterly decompression window. You are not scheduling vacation as reward. You are scheduling fallow as structural requirement.

STEP SEVEN: PLAN FOR CONSTRAINT

Real life will interrupt you. Include a constraint clause: when constraint increases, I will not add new offerings. I will tighten gates and protect micro-return. This prevents the most common burnout reaction: pressure increases, so you add more.

• • •

REFLECTION

What shape does your year actually want to take—Two-Harvest, Caregiving, Stewardship, or Initiation? Which shape have you been forcing it into instead?

Which domain is the primary offering domain this year? What changes when you name it honestly?

Where in your year have you scheduled offerings without scheduling the Return that would make them sustainable?

What is the one threshold you most need to install before the next season turns?

What constraint clause does your year need—the predecided rule that keeps a hard season from becoming collapse?

CHAPTER 11

WHEN THE WHEEL DOESN'T FIT

Any framework worth trusting should be honest about its limits. The Wheel of the Year offers a pattern—and that pattern can illuminate a great deal. But patterns are not prisons, and cosmology is not a diagnostic manual. There are lives and circumstances where the four-fold arc requires adaptation, qualification, or humility.

This chapter names some of those circumstances—not to undermine the Wheel, but to strengthen it. A framework that cannot hold complexity becomes another form of collapsed time: one more system telling you that your experience is wrong because it does not match the model.

CHRONIC ILLNESS AND DISABILITY

The Wheel assumes that seasons turn. But for people living with chronic illness, disability, or long-term pain, the experience is often not cyclical—it is a sustained condition with its own logic. Return may not lead to Becoming. Offering may be limited in ways that feel permanent rather than seasonal.

Fallow may not restore what has been lost.

This does not mean the Wheel is useless here. It means the Wheel must be applied with smaller increments and gentler expectations. A person with a chronic condition may find that the arc operates within a single day rather than across a year: a morning of capacity, an afternoon of governance, an evening of return. The principle remains—gates, timing, the refusal to extract endlessly—but the scale changes.

What the Wheel can still offer in these circumstances is this: the insistence that your limits are not moral failures. The refusal to treat perpetual offering as devotion.

ECONOMIC PRECARITY

The Wheel counsels Return. But for people living in economic precarity—paycheck to paycheck, unstable housing, caregiving without support—the question "Where can you withdraw?" can sound tone-deaf.

This deserves acknowledgment rather than evasion. The Wheel does not pretend that everyone has equal access to rest. What it does name is this: the inability to return is itself a timing wound—not a personal one, but a structural one. When an economy denies fallow to the people who need it most, that is a collective violation of seasonal order.

In these circumstances, the Wheel is not asking you to perform a return you cannot afford. It is naming the injury clearly—and offering the smallest possible acts of timing as resistance: a ten-minute concealment window, a refusal to add guilt to exhaustion, the recognition that you deserve seasons even when systems deny them.

NEURODIVERGENCE AND RHYTHM

The Wheel speaks in rhythms. But for some people—those with ADHD, autism, or other neurodivergent patterns—rhythm itself works differently. Hyperfocus is not the same as Offering. Executive function collapse is not the same as Return. The internal clock may not follow seasons in any predictable way.

The Wheel can still be useful here, but it needs to be adapted. A neurodivergent person might find that Becoming and Offering alternate rapidly rather than in long seasons. They might find that Authority—the governance of attention and commitments—requires external supports that the Wheel does not specify.

They might find that Return looks like stimulation and novelty rather than quiet and withdrawal.

The principle remains: you cannot extract from yourself endlessly. But the shape of the arc may need to be yours, not the one described in any book —including this one.

GRIEF THAT DOES NOT TURN

Some grief is seasonal. You descend, you dwell in darkness, and eventually something begins to form again. But some grief does not follow the arc. The loss of a child, the end of a world, the betrayal that restructures identity—these can create a kind of permanent winter that does not serve as Becoming. It simply is.

The Wheel does not need to claim that all grief is cyclical. What it can offer is a refusal to rush the timeline. If the Wheel teaches anything, it teaches that forcing seasons is itself a violence. Some grief asks you to stay where you are—not as a violation of the arc, but as a recognition that this particular winter has its own duration, and it is not yours to shorten.

WHEN SYSTEMIC HARM IS THE PROBLEM

The Wheel speaks to individual timing. But burnout is not always an individual problem. When the source of extraction is racism, poverty, ableism, misogyny, or institutional violence, "restore your arc" is not a sufficient answer.

This book does not pretend to solve systemic harm through personal cosmology. What it can do is refuse to blame individuals for structural extraction. And it can name the sacred right of every person to live inside seasons—not as a privilege, but as a requirement of being alive.

If the Wheel is honest, it must acknowledge that the timing wound is not distributed equally. Some people have more access to Return than others. Some people have been denied Becoming for generations. And for some—those in incarceration, institutional care, domestic abuse, or exploitative labor—timing is not merely collapsed but imposed: their seasons are controlled by others, and the wound is not a matter of personal habit but of captivity. Naming this is not a departure from the Wheel's theology. It is its natural consequence: if seasonal order is sacred, then the denial of seasons is profane.

THE FRAMEWORK AS HEURISTIC, NOT LAW

Throughout this book, I have used the language of law, cosmology, and sacred order. I have done this because weak language does not heal strong wounds. The Wheel needed to be presented with enough weight to counter the enormous pressure of collapsed time.

But I want to be transparent about the claim: the fourfold arc is a heuristic—a pattern that reveals what might otherwise remain invisible. It is offered as cosmology because cosmology is how humans make sense of time. But it is not a natural law in the way that gravity is. It is a framework, drawn from myth and season and observation, that invites you to see your life differently.

If it helps, use it. If parts of it do not fit, trust that. The Wheel is not a cage. It is a trellis—and a trellis is only useful if the living thing it supports can grow in its own shape.

REFLECTION

Where in your life does the Wheel fit well? Where does it need adaptation?

Have you been blaming yourself for a timing wound that is partly structural—economic, medical, systemic?

What scale does the arc operate on in your life: yearly, monthly, daily?

Where might the framework be pushing you toward a season you can't genuinely enter, and what would honest acknowledgment look like?

CHAPTER 12

THE RETURN YOU KEEP

Most people do not lack the ability to rest. They lack the ability to return.

They can stop for a weekend, take a vacation, sleep late, disappear for a day, and still come back to the same collapsed time with the same internal pressure humming underneath it. The pause relieves symptoms, but it does not restore the pattern. It does not rebuild gates. It does not change the reflex to prove.

This chapter is about a different kind of renewal. A renewal that does not depend on collapse. A renewal that does not require permission. A renewal that returns you to sacred timing again and again.

RENEWAL AS PRACTICE, NOT RESCUE

To keep Return, you must stop treating it as a reward. Reward implies earning. Earning implies proving.

Proving implies collapsed time.

Return is not a reward. It is a requirement of viability. And therefore, it must be practiced like any other essential condition: regularly, imperfectly, without drama.

Think of Return the way you think of sleep—not as a luxury, but as something your life is built around because without it, you cannot live. The Return you keep is the Return you do not negotiate every time.

A Closing Rite

Collapsed time hates endings. It keeps tasks open, conversations unresolved, obligations ambiguous, and attention hooked. A closing rite is a small act that deliberately creates an ending. Not for aesthetics. For closure. You can use it daily, weekly, or at the end of an offering season.

Close the gate. A physical action: shut the laptop, turn off the light, wash your hands, step outside. Let the body feel an ending.

Enter Return deliberately. "I am released." or "Now, I return."

A closing rite does not require you to feel calm. It requires you to enact a gate. Over time, the nervous system learns that the day has an end that is not collapse.

A Vow of Timing

Most burnout is caused by a broken ethic—one you inherited from collapsed time: prove, produce, endure, stay available, keep going. To keep Return, you need a different ethic. Not a set of goals, but a vow—something you can come back to when you are tempted to violate time again.

I will not offer from the seed.

I will not confuse urgency with ripeness.

I will build gates around my giving.

I will treat Return as law, not reward.

I will not require collapse to justify rest.

I will come back again when I drift.

This vow is not moralism. It is protection. It does not ask you to be perfect. It asks you to stop sanctifying violations of viability.

THE RETURN PROTOCOL

Even with a rhythm rule and a yearly plan, there will be weeks when the Wheel is violated. So you need a way to come back quickly—without shame spirals, without dramatic resets.

Step 1: Locate the violation. Which violation is active? Premature sacrifice, urgency, forced visibility, or Return denied? Name one. Naming breaks the spell.

Step 2: Restore one gate within 24 hours. Do not repair everything. A stop-time. A concealment window. A canceled obligation. Ten minutes of real return. Re-establish the pattern somewhere immediately.

Step 3: Protect the next Return. Return is kept by repetition. Protect the next Return—tonight, tomorrow, this weekend—before the week steals it again.

THE SPIRITUAL MEANING OF COMING BACK

Many people treat drift as evidence that they are incapable of change. They think: I always end up here. I always overgive. I always collapse.

But in the Wheel's cosmology, coming back is not failure. It is devotion. Devotion, in this book, has never meant depletion. It has meant lawful return.

To come back again and again—quietly, without drama—is to refuse the theology of collapsed time. It is to refuse the demand to be limitless. It is to live under a different order.

The God does not always remain visible. He does not always remain in offering. He does not always remain crowned. He returns.

And so can you.

REFLECTION

What do you currently treat as renewal—and does it actually restore the pattern, or only provide temporary relief?

What is one closing rite you can practice to give your life real endings?

Which line of the vow of timing do you resist most—and what fear is beneath that resistance?

When you drift into collapsed time, which gate can you restore within 24 hours?

What would it mean to treat coming back as devotion—renewal as practice, not rescue?

The Season Finder

Use this diagnostic once a week or whenever you feel misaligned. It takes ten minutes.

Step 1: Name Your Global Season

Read the four descriptions below. Circle the one that most closely matches your overall condition right now—not the one you wish were true, but the one that is true.

Becoming: Something is forming but not yet ready. I am absorbing more than producing. Visibility feels premature. I need protection, not exposure.

Authority: Things are steady but demanding. I am holding a lot in place. I need governance, limits, and containment—not new projects.

Offering: Something is ripe. I am actively giving, delivering, creating, or producing outwardly. The work is real, but it needs a gate.

Return: I am depleted, withdrawn, or asking for rest. My system is signaling that demand must decrease. I need fallow, not more effort.

My global season right now:

Step 2: Map Your Domains

List your four to six primary life domains (examples: work, parenting, marriage/partnership, body/health, home/logistics, creativity/calling, community/social life).

For each domain, write:

The domain:

Its current season: Becoming / Authority / Offering / Return

Current demand in one sentence:

Right posture: Protect / Govern / Offer with a gate / Withdraw

One repair:

STEP 3: CHECK THE PATTERN

Count how many domains are in expansion. If more than two, identify the one that can shift into preservation this week.

If Return is absent from every domain, that is the most urgent repair.

Two Completed Personal Wheel Plans

Example 1: The Caregiving Year

Lena is 38. She has two children under six, a stable but unexciting job, and a mother recovering from surgery. Her husband works long hours.

Year shape: Caregiving Year. One primary offering domain (work); everything else in governance and micro-return.

Primary offering domain: Work (income is non-negotiable).

Offerings This Year:

1. Maintain current job performance without pursuing promotion.
2. Support mother's recovery through spring
3. No third offering.

Thresholds: No evening work past 8 pm. No new volunteer commitments. No hosting holidays this year.

Planned Return:

Weekly: Saturday morning alone (husband covers kids).

Monthly: One full day off with no caregiving or household labor.

Seasonal: Two weeks of simplified routine in August (no camps, no enrichment, minimal cooking).

Constraint clause: If mother's recovery stalls or a child gets sick, I drop all social obligations and simplify meals to five rotating dinners. I do not add guilt.

EXAMPLE 2: THE TWO-HARVEST YEAR

Marcus is 44, self-employed as a consultant, partnered with no children. He is recovering from a burnout collapse eighteen months ago.

Year shape: Two-Harvest Year. Two offering seasons with a deliberate fallow between them.

Primary offering domain: Consulting practice.

OFFERINGS THIS YEAR:

• Spring client engagement season (March–May).

• Fall workshop series (September–November). No summer offerings. No December offerings.

Thresholds: Maximum three active clients at once. No travel more than two weeks per month.

Partnership moves to Authority during offering seasons (clear logistics, no deep processing, protect each other's sleep).

PLANNED RETURN:

Weekly: Sundays are completely unscheduled.

Seasonal: June–August is a consolidation and fallow period—no new business development, existing clients only, reduced hours. December is full Return—no work.

Constraint clause: If a major unexpected demand arises (health crisis, family emergency), I cancel the fall workshop series rather than running both offerings under strain. One harvest is enough.

THE WEEKLY WHEEL LEDGER

Use this weekly. It takes ten minutes. The goal is not to fix your life in one sitting. The goal is to stop acting blindly from a season that is not yours.

Date:

Global season this week:

Domain 1:

Season:

Demand:

Posture:

One repair:

Domain 2:

Season:

Demand:

Posture:

One repair:

Domain 3:

Season:

Demand:

Posture:

One repair:

Domain 4:

Season:

Demand:

Posture:

One repair:

Domain 5:

Season:

Demand:

Posture:

One repair:

Domain 6:

Season:

Demand:

Posture:

One repair:

How many domains are in expansion?

Where is Return absent?

What is the one violation I will stop this week?

What is the one gate I will protect?

THE CLOSING RITE AND VOW OF TIMING

These two texts are offered as ritual. They are meant to be used—spoken, repeated, returned to. Print this page. Post it where you will see it. Let the words become familiar enough that they arrive when you need them.

THE CLOSING RITE

Use daily, weekly, or at the end of an offering season:

Name what was offered. One sentence.

Name what is complete. Even if only one thing.

Name what is not yours to carry overnight.

Close the gate—a physical action: shut the laptop, turn off the light, wash your hands, step outside.

Enter Return deliberately: "I am released." Or: "Now, I return."

THE VOW OF TIMING

I will not offer from the seed. I will not confuse urgency with ripeness.

I will build gates around my giving.

I will treat Return as law, not reward.

I will not require collapse to justify rest.

I will come back again when I drift.

APPENDIX E

WORKS IN CONVERSATION

This book does not exist in isolation. The following texts have informed, accompanied, or challenged the thinking that shaped it. They are offered as companions—not prerequisites—for readers who want to go deeper.

ON BURNOUT AND THE BODY

Emily Nagoski and Amelia Nagoski, *Burnout: The Secret to Unlocking the Stress Cycle*. The clearest available account of how stress lives in the body and how to complete the stress cycle. Pairs well with this book's theological frame—they name the biology; we name the cosmology.

Oliver Burkeman, *Four Thousand Weeks: Time Management for Mortals*. A secular meditation on finitude and the impossibility of "getting on top of everything."

ON SACRED TIME AND SABBATH

Wayne Muller, *Sabbath: Restoring the Sacred Rhythm of Rest*. The closest non-Pagan companion to this book. Muller writes from a broadly interfaith perspective about the violence of overwork and the sacredness of stopping. If the Wheel speaks your language, Muller speaks a neighboring dialect.

John Mark Comer, *The Ruthless Elimination of Hurry*. A Christian account of why busyness is a spiritual emergency. Useful for readers who want to see how other traditions name the same injury.

ON THE WHEEL OF THE YEAR

Kristi Hall, *Imbolc: A Theology of Winter and the Making of Spring*. The companion volume to this book. Where The Timing Wound applies the God's arc as a diagnostic framework for burnout, the Imbolc book enters a single threshold on the Wheel and explores it devotionally—through land, deity, Tarot, and the discipline of carrying what winter has not yet released. For readers who want the mythic depth beneath the practical tools.

Ronald Hutton, *The Stations of the Sun*. A careful historical study of British seasonal customs. Essential reading for understanding what the Wheel of the Year is and is not as a historical phenomenon.

Ronald Hutton, *The Triumph of the Moon*. The definitive history of modern Pagan witchcraft in Britain. Provides the context for how the Wheel became a liturgical structure.

Mircea Eliade, *The Sacred and the Profane*. A foundational exploration of sacred time and cyclical religious imagination. The distinction between sacred and profane time that runs through this book owes a debt to Eliade's framework.

Emma Restall Orr, *The Wakeful World*. A philosophical and theological reflection from within contemporary Druidry that treats land and deity as relational presences rather than metaphors.

This book stands at the intersection of contemporary Pagan theology and the lived experience of burnout and spiritual fatigue. The interpretations offered here are the author's own. They are offered as a framework for renewal, not as clinical guidance.

Continuing the Work

Imbolc: A Theology of Winter and the Making of Spring

Where *The Timing Wound* applies the God's arc diagnostically — as a framework for naming what has gone wrong with how modern life treats time — *Imbolc* enters a single threshold on the Wheel and stays there. It is a devotional study of the season when what was seeded in winter has not yet ripened into spring, and the discipline required is to keep carrying what cannot yet be released. For readers who want the mythic depth beneath the diagnostic.

Available in paperback, ebook, and audiobook.

Turn: A Theological Library for the Wheel of the Year

A companion digital library to the Turn book series, treating each sabbat as a threshold with its own theology, practice, and structure. *Beltane* is currently available and complete. Additional sabbats are released as their volumes are written; the library will ultimately hold all eight thresholds. For readers who want to live inside one season at a time rather than survey the whole Wheel.

Hours: A Theology of Day and Night

A library on the sacred structure of the daily cycle — the hours as thresholds, the turning from night to day and back again. Complete, with a companion ebook available. For readers who found the Wheel's argument persuasive and want to apply the same theological reading to the time-scale inside a single day.

ARCANA: A CONTEMPLATIVE TAROT STUDY

A contemplative tarot study for practitioners who want more than surface meanings. Built for depth, designed for return. Each card is opened through theology, myth, image, meditation, and journaling practice. *In development.*

• • •

GRIST

The home for everything above, including the forthcoming companion resources for *The Timing Wound* — a digital workbook, printable guides, and a library extension of the material in this book.

grist.theology

About the Author

Kristi Hall has studied and practiced polytheism in various forms for decades. She practices alone, unaffiliated with any group or established tradition.

Her work comes from her own reflection on these subjects over many years, and from the wish to share those reflections — the questions, the arguments, the half-formed intuitions — so that the conversation can continue. She writes for practitioners who want the framework beneath the practice, and the theology beneath the framework.

She is the founder of Grist, a publishing and library imprint for polytheist theology. She lives and writes in the United States.